SUNNY
SIDE UP

JENNIFER L. HOLM & MATTHEW HOLM
WITH COLOR BY LARK PIEN

graphix
AN IMPRINT OF
SCHOLASTIC

All rights reserved. Published by Graphix, an imprint of Scholastic Inc., *Publishers since 1920.* SCHOLASTIC, GRAPHIX, and associated logos are trademarks and/or registered trademarks of Scholastic Inc.

The publisher does not have any control over and does not assume any responsibility for author or third-party websites or their content.

ISBN 978-0-545-89934-5

10 9 8 7 6 5 4 3 2 1   15 16 17 18 19

Printed in Singapore 46
First printing 2015
Edited by David Levithan
Lettering by Fawn Lau
Color by Lark Pien
Book design by Phil Falco
Creative Director: David Saylor

For Gramps

CHAPTER ONE:
Sunshine State

August 1976

West Palm Beach, Fla.

SKTTCHH!

7

So what do you think of Bertha? I splurged!

Got all the bells and whistles to impress the ladies.

NEW!

8-TRACK PLAYER!

1976! "BERTHA!" 200 HORSE-POWER!

Dale would love this car.

CHAPTER TWO:
Fifty-Five and Over

18

Ewww...

Here ya go, hon.

Now make sure you have that with you at all times.

Okay.

PINE PALMS

Visitor# _211_

Name: _SUNSHINE LEWIN_

Age: _10_

Issued: _AUGUST 8, 1976_

Expires: _SEPTEMB_

Boy, your baby brother sure cries a lot.

Teddy hates taking naps.

Does my hair look like Dorothy Hamill's at all?

SKATING QUEEN DOROTHY HAMILL

Dorothy

The Wedge!

I think it's supposed to be more of a wedge in the back.

NOT A WEDGE

26

Brother?

WAAHHHH!

Uh, yeah!

One that doesn't cry all the time!

Hopefully he won't cry all summer.

I almost forgot!

I'm allowed to bring a friend when we go on vacation at the shore in August!

My mom's going to call your mom today to ask her!

29

CHAPTER FOUR:
Hide-a-Bed

KNOCK, KNOCK!

That'll be the girls!

There are other kids visiting?

"THE GIRLS!"

I'm Teezy!

I'm Ethel!

You must be Sunny!

Your grandfather's told us all about you!

35

That evening.

CHAPTER FIVE:
Adult Swim

There she is!

How was the hide-a-bed? Sleep well?

YAWN

I have BIG PLANS for today!

Really?

The day after that.

TWEET!

SKIDDD!

I need to see your pass.

Uh...

You can't use the pool without a **VISITOR PASS.**

That's the rule.

You don't look ten.

I don't?

Florida, August 1976

THUNK!

I quit smoking.

You did?

My doctor's worried about my cough.

Thinks it's emphysema and that I shouldn't smoke anymore.

That afternoon.

Pine Palms Clubhouse

I need to pay my greens fees.

Here's some change for a soda. It might take a while.

CLICK!

CLICK!

Give it a good kick.

It gets stuck.

WHUNK!

CLUNK!

Thanks.

FSST!

What's Swamp Thing?

SIP!

CHAPTER SEVEN:
Big Al

What do you want to do?

Let's go swimming at the pool.

I can't. I don't have a visitor pass.

Oh. Right.

Let's go pick up golf balls from the course.

Why?

Because the guy at the pro shop pays me a nickel a ball.

A little later.

WHIZZZ!!

PERLUNK!

Guess that one's gone.

WHIRRR....

We have 19 balls!

SPLISH

Sunny?

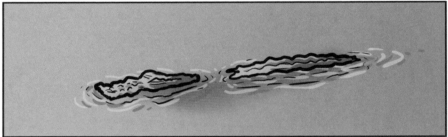

FLING!

ZIP!

PANT! GASP!

WHEEZE!

THWIPP!

This is really good.

Spider-Man's great.

SPIDER-MAN!
Real name is Peter Parker
Bitten by a spider and got its POWERS!
Can shoot webs from wrists!
Has "Spider" sense!
I like that he's a teenager. It makes him seem real.
And he can shoot webs from his wrists!

CHAPTER NINE:
Lunch Box

FITTING
ROOMS

Come on,
Sunny. Pick
one.

I need to
get your brother
down for a nap.

But I have to get the perfect one or else I won't have a good year at school.

FLASH!

SNAP!

Have a great first day of school!

Jonathan King?

Here.

Sunshine Lewin?

Here!

Are you related to Dale Lewin, by any chance?

He's my big brother!

I had your brother
last year when I taught
eleventh grade.

SCRIBBLE

CHAPTER TEN:
Early Bird Special

There you are! I'm taking you and the girls out to dinner. Better hurry up and get dressed.

?

Isn't it a little early?

Early? It's already 4:00! We need to be on the road by 4:15!

Punch it, Pat!

Or we'll be late!

93

I forgot to get ambrosia salad.

Be back in a sec.

Now, do you have any brothers or sisters?

Uh, my brother Teddy is one.

You live near Valley Forge?

It must have been a big deal with the Bicentennial.

NOD

94

BICENTENNIAL!

America's 200th birthday!

FREEDOM TRAIN!

PAINTED FIRE HYDRANTS!

CONESTOGA WAGONS!

PEOPLE DRESSING IN WOOLEN COSTUMES!

JELL-O SALADS MADE WITH RED, WHITE, AND BLUE!

Were there fireworks?

Yes.

After dinner.

I'll just go pull the car around for you ladies.

Put the roll in your purse!

Why?

In case you get hungry later!

Don't forget the butter!

Later.

SQUEAK!

CLICK

MUNCH
MUNCH

SQUEAK!
SQUEAK!

CHAPTER ELEVEN:
Ice Cream

Wait! The grocery store is that way!

We'll stop on our way home.

Way home from what?

Teaching you to drive.

You two were sure gone a long time getting a gallon of milk.

You weren't hanging out with that Sladek boy, were you? He's no good.

Nah! Sunny wanted some ice cream so I took her out to the Dairy Barn.

Right, Sunny?

Yeah. Chocolate!

Ice cream. Hmm.

Hey—not so fast.

Fork over my change, mister.

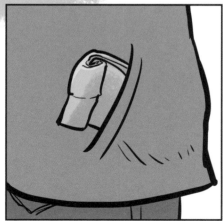

CHAPTER TWELVE:
Heroes

I thought cats weren't allowed at Pine Palms.

Lots of the old ladies have them anyway.

I feel kind of bad that we took the dollar from that old lady.

It was a lot easier than looking for golf balls.

CHAPTER THIRTEEN:
Pompeii

April 1976

Pennsylvania

VENICE
TO
WILMOT,
JOHN

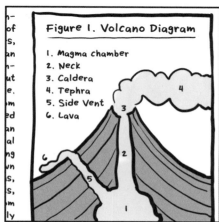

Figure 1. Volcano Diagram

1. Magma chamber
2. Neck
3. Caldera
4. Tephra
5. Side Vent
6. Lava

NOTABLE VOLCANOES

Pompeii, Italy, AD 79. The ancient Roman city of POMPEII was destroyed by the eruption of the volcano VESUVIUS. Thousands were buried under a hail of ash, preserving them where they fell.

PLATES 1–3. Plaster casts of eruption victims

Later.

How was the office today?

SLAM!

The new receptionist doesn't know how to work the phones.

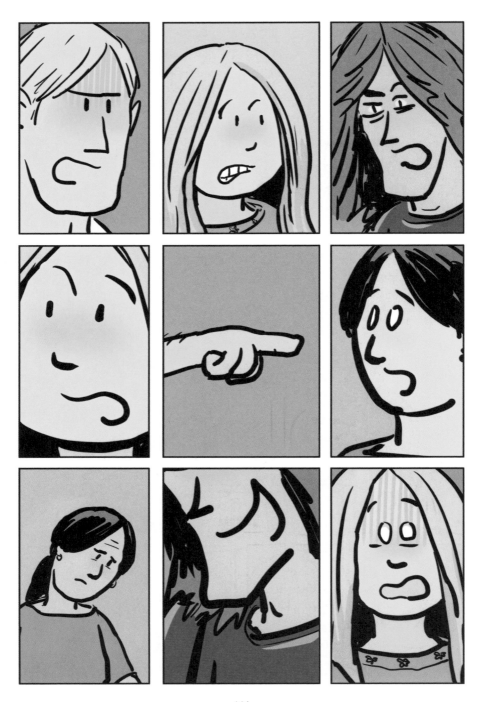

HAVE YOU HEARD ABOUT POMPEII?

I'm doing this report on volcanoes and Pompeii was this huge volcano that erupted and froze everybody in the ash like statues!

Of course. That was a very famous eruption.

This is good meat loaf, Mom.

Your father's favorite.

RATTLE
RATTLE

RALEIGH

SUPERMAN

SECRET IDENTITY IS **CLARK KENT!**

CAN **FLY!**

WORKS FOR THE DAILY PLANET NEWSPAPER!

BORN ON ANOTHER **PLANET!**

That's the superpower I'd want! Wouldn't that be cool? To be able to fly?

I guess.

Well, what superpower would you want?

Uh...

Strength? Speed? Ability to talk to dolphins?

Ability to talk to dolphins?

Yeah! It's super useful if you're in the ocean!

So. What superpower would you want?

Invisibility.

May 1976

Pennsylvania

Did you start your book report yet?

Not yet, but I read the book.

What was it?

The Black Cauldron. It's the best book I've ever read. It's about—

SCREECH!!

SCREE!

FLING!

SMASH!

HA HA HA!

HA HA HA HA HA!

Was that your brother?

CHAPTER FIFTEEN:
Lost

May 1976

Dinner's almost ready.

Your dad has a late meeting, so we'll eat without him.

Pennsylvania

Can you please go find Dale?

Sure, Mom!

Dale!

Dale!

140

You didn't see anything, did you, Sunny?

(SWALLOW)

No. I didn't see a thing.

Two hours later.

HOLE 19

This place is so big! She could be anywhere!

PUTT PUTT PUTT

But—but—but—I don't know how to drive!

I've got this.

PUTT
PUTT

Pine Palms

RRRUMMBLE!

VROOOOM...

Are you waiting for the bus?

Yes. The number ten bus to Hoboken.

Mickey will be waiting for me.

Where's Hoboken?

In New Jersey, of course!

Ooh! Look, a new *Swamp Thing!*

SWAMP THING

!KIDS MICS WH CC ENT

PRESCRIP

So you like Swamp Thing now?

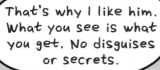

I think he's my favorite.

Really? But he doesn't even have a costume. He doesn't even have a cape!

13

That's why I like him. What you see is what you get. No disguises or secrets.

If you say so.

Oh yeah.

My mami wants to know if you and your grandfather would like to come over for dinner tomorrow night.

Flowers! How lovely! You didn't have to, Mister Hearn.

Please, call me Pat.

COUGH!

HACK!

HACK!
HACK!
HACK!

Are you a doctor?

A chemist. Well, I **was** a chemist. Back in Cuba.

Here, it's not so easy. No papers...

Hey, Papi. You're kind of like Batman.

You're really a chemist, but your secret identity is a gardener.

Ha-ha! I think I'd rather have my secret identity be a millionaire like Bruce Wayne.

Would you like to see my library?

Whoa.

PRINCE VALIANT – VOL. 3
PRINCE VALIANT – VOL. 2
PRINCE VALIANT – VOL. 1
FLASH GORDON
TERRY AND THE PIRATES

THE UNSINKABLE CHARLIE BROWN
YOU CAN DO IT, CHARLIE BROWN
B.C. STRIKES BACK   JOHNNY HART
TAKE A BOW, B.C.   JOHNNY HART

This is my other passion.

I've never seen so many comics in my whole life!

CHAPTER EIGHTEEN:
SMASH!

HULK SMASH!

I don't understand the Hulk.

What's to understand? He's big and green.

CHAPTER NINETEEN:
Fireworks

July 4, 1976

Pennsylvania

That evening.

Valley Forge Park

Where have you been? You were supposed to be here hours ago.

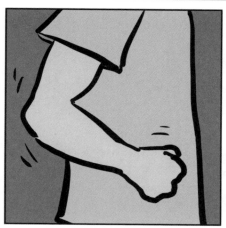

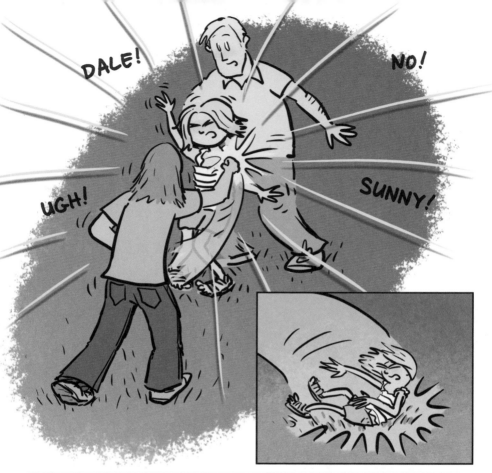

BOOM!

POP!

BOOM!

CHAPTER TWENTY:
Volcano

SIGH

Are we going shopping for new swimsuits for the beach today?

Sunny, I have some bad news. We won't be going to the beach house after all.

Your dad thinks it's best that we cancel the trip.

August 1976

Florida

COUGH!
HACK!
COUGH!

SIGH.

You up, old girl?

COUGH!

Yeah.

SIGH

SQUEAK!

FOOM!

It's just that I don't want to keep any more secrets.

You don't have to keep secrets.

I don't?

SHAKE SHAKE

The hide-a-bed's awful!

It's uncomfortable and lumpy and it squeaks and I can't sleep!

I hate it! It's the worst thing ever!

That's why Mom and Dad sent me down here.

I made everything worse at July Fourth. I got Dale in even bigger trouble!

Oh, old girl. You didn't make anything worse.

SHAKE

SHAKE

But, but—

Your parents are trying to get your brother help and they don't want you to see that, because it isn't going to be pretty.

Dale has some big problems.

But why is he like this? Why can't he just stop and be the old Dale again?

Why?????

SIGH

I don't know, old girl.

But I do know that it's not up to **YOU** to fix him and it's not **YOUR** fault. Okay?

SNIFF

Okay.

I promise you. No more hiding cigarettes—

Or **smoking** them—

Or smoking them.

Now let's see about this hide-a-bed of yours.

CHAPTER TWENTY-ONE:
Polaroid Moment

CREEEAK!

You want to do the honors?

DUMPSTER FOR RESIDENT USE ONLY

SWISH!

A few days later.

Hey, old girl!

Keep your sunny side up!

A NOTE FROM JENNIFER L. HOLM & MATTHEW HOLM

Sometimes it's hard to be a kid. It can be even harder when someone you love has a drug or alcohol abuse problem.

Like Sunny, we had a close relative who had serious issues with substance abuse. As children, we were bystanders to this behavior and yet it affected our whole world. It made us feel ashamed and embarrassed and scared and sad. Most of all, it was something that we felt we had to keep secret.

We wrote this book so that young readers who are facing these same problems today don't feel ashamed like we did. When someone in a family struggles with substance abuse, the whole family struggles. It's okay to feel sad and confused and to need some help. And it's definitely okay to talk about it.

If you find yourself in a situation like Sunny, don't be scared. Reach out to family members and teachers and school counselors. They'll be able to help you find the right resources so that you can keep your sunny side up.

ACKNOWLEDGMENTS

We would like to thank all the incredible people who helped Sunny find her way onto the page. With special thanks to David Levithan, Phil Falco, Lark Pien, Fawn Lau, Cyndi Koon, Ed Masessa, Sheila Marie Everett, Lizette Serrano, Elizabeth Krych, and Alexandria Terry. And for incredible encouragement, we are eternally grateful to Jill Grinberg, Shannon Rosa, Myly Posse, Larry Marder, and our readers everywhere.

JENNIFER L. HOLM & MATTHEW HOLM are the award-winning brother-sister team behind the Babymouse and Squish series. Jennifer is also the author of many acclaimed novels, including three Newbery Honor books and the NEW YORK TIMES bestseller THE FOURTEENTH GOLDFISH. SUNNY SIDE UP is a semi-autobiographical book inspired by their childhood.

LARK PIEN is an indie cartoonist from Oakland, California. She has published many comics and is the colorist for Printz Award winner AMERICAN BORN CHINESE, and BOXERS & SAINTS. Her characters Long Tail Kitty and Mr. Elephanter have been adapted into children's books. She holds the world's tiniest rainbow, which is way heavier than it looks. www.larkpien.blogspot.com